M000087037

ISBN-13: 9781693947797

Cover and map design: Avigail Litvak

Ani Ve-Ami Jewish Living Education
http://ani-ve-ami.com/
aniveami@gmail.com

Ani Ve-ami Curriculum Guide: Talmud

by Yehudis Litvak

Table of Contents

Foreword

Welcome to the Ani Ve-Ami Curriculum! This guide will help you navigate the curriculum and customize it to best fit your family's needs.

This guide covers:
- History and structure of Mishna and Gemara
- Jewish history
- Jewish literature
- Grammar
- Jewish music
- Jewish art
- Geography

Additional materials needed:
- notebook (for each child)
- drawing paper
- pens, pencils, crayons

The books for required and additional reading, as well as recommended art, music, and poetry are listed in Appendix A.

To complete the curriculum, you will need:
- Ani Ve-Ami Jewish Year Curriculum Guide
- Weekly Parsha book(s) of your choice (see ani-ve-ami.com for recommendations)
- *The Story of the World* Volume 1 (this time period is covered in chapters 25 - 42; you can skip chapter 38, since this material is covered in Jewish history) and its accompanying Activity Book OR *The History of the Ancient World* Volume 1 (this time period covers part 5) and its accompanying Study Guide; books listed on the ani-ve-ami.com website on the page for this time period (you may be able to borrow these books from your local library)
- a math curriculum of your choice (see ani-ve-ami.com for recommendations)
- a science curriculum of your choice (see ani-ve-ami.com for recommendations)
- a Hebrew language curriculum of your choice, as well as textual study resources, if desired (see ani-ve-ami.com for recommendations)

This guide breaks up the school year into ten month-long units. While most homeschoolers will begin using this curriculum in September, some families might structure their school year differently, or begin Ani Ve-Ami mid-year. For this reason, the months are numbered, but not named. It is up to each family to decide how the monthly breakdown corresponds to their own schedule.

In addition, some families may choose to go through the curriculum at a quicker pace, while others may find it more effective to slow down and spend more than a month on each unit. Perhaps your children are especially interested in a specific unit, or perhaps, you have a child with special needs who takes longer to absorb the material, or perhaps your family loves to travel or is otherwise too busy to fit everything in this guide into a tight schedule. That's perfectly fine. There is no right or wrong way to do this. This curriculum is meant to be adjusted to your family's unique needs.

This guide is intended for the whole family. The guidelines below describe how to use it for multiple children of different ages. Each child will be working on their own level, while at the same time participating in relevant family activities.

For each monthly unit, this guide offers a brief summary, as well as recommended reading and, sometimes, additional reading. The additional reading will sometimes take longer and overlap with the next monthly unit. Don't worry — some months don't have additional reading, and you won't fall behind.

If your children are young, you might want to omit the additional reading. If you have both older and younger children, you might use the recommended reading as a read aloud for the whole family and the additional reading as independent reading for your older children. If all your children are older, you can use both recommended and additional reading as read alouds, or you might assign some of either recommended or additional reading to your children to read independently. Feel free to experiment and see what works best for your family.

The monthly units also introduce your children to Jewish or Talmud-themed art and music, with selections for each month that are relevant to the time period, either in content or because it was produced in that time period.

Unlike our other curriculum guides, this one does not include Jewish poetry, since not much Jewish poetry was written in the Talmud time period. There are various reasons for this. During the Talmud time period, and especially after the destruction of the Second Temple, Jewish life transitioned from Temple-centered to Torah-centered. Jewish sages of the time codified and committed to writing large parts of the Oral Torah. Their creativity was directed towards this massive undertaking, which ensured the survival of Judaism for all future generations. While the texts of Mishna and Gemara are very different from the poetic style of the Tanach or from Jewish medieval poetry, they nevertheless follow their own rhythm and highlight the beauty of the Jewish tradition in their unique style. As at other times in Jewish history, the Jews of the Talmud time period saw and valued beauty, expressing it in the way that spoke to their generation.

Each monthly unit contains three or four weekly units. Each weekly unit is based on a short story or book excerpt set in the times of the Talmud or a passage from the Talmud itself. In the beginning of the week, you can read the story or passage aloud to your children. In the following days, each of your children will do narration and copy work or dictation on the story or passage.

Depending on the age of the child, narration could be oral, pictorial, or written. For more on narration, see the How It Works section of the Ani Ve-Ami website.

Each weekly unit contains a paragraph for copy work or dictation and a grammar exercise based on that paragraph. A younger child should only copy a sentence or two. An older child should copy the whole paragraph and do the grammar exercise that accompanies it. For more on copy work and dictation, see the How It Works section of the Ani Ve-Ami website.

The monthly units also contain maps and directions for map work. We recommend that you make a copy of the map for each of your children and let them do the map work on their own level, with your help if necessary.

Month 1

Overview

This is the first month of the homeschooling year. If you are beginning your year in the fall, you will be busy getting ready for the Jewish holidays of the month of *Tishrei* (see our *Jewish Year Curriculum Guide* for more details).

Even if you begin your year in a different month, it might take you time to get into a routine, or you might want to review what you covered in the previous year. Therefore, for this month, we prepared only three weeks of learning. As always, if you find yourself with extra time, please see our recommendations for additional reading.

Focus of the month: beginning of the Second Temple period
Events: the Great Assembly; sealing the Tanach; canonized prayers and blessings
Time period: years 3410 - 3460 on the Jewish calendar (years 349 - 301 BCE)

Brief summary of the time period:
The Land of Judea, with its capital in Jerusalem, is part of the Persian Empire. The Jews worship in the newly rebuilt Temple and rebuild Jewish life. The Great Assembly, consisting of

the greatest Jewish sages of the time, makes the final determination of what is to be included in the Tanach. From then on, no more books are added to the Tanach. The Great Assembly also canonizes the text of the prayers, as well as blessings.

Then Alexander the Great conquers Judea, among many other lands. The Persian Empire falls, and the Greeks become the dominant force in the world. Thus begins the encounter between the Jews and the Greeks.

Materials

Recommended reading for this month:
   The Miracles of Chanukah Then and Now by Genendel Krohn, Prologue

Weekly reading:
   Week 1: *True Gift*, by Yehudis Litvak
   Week 2: *In Every Generation*, by Yehudis Litvak
   Week 3: *Brotherly Love*, by Yehudis Litvak

Grammar: *A Journey Through Grammar Land, Parts 1 and 2* by Jones & Jensen
   Chapters 1: The Naming Part (alias Subject); and 2: Namers (alias Nouns)

Geography:
   Map of Greece, Macedonia, Judea, and Persia
   Map work: trace Alexander's route of conquest; color in Judea; circle Jerusalem

Music: *Somachti* by Shalsheles (song # 4 in the album *Connections;* available at https://mostlymusic.com/products/connections)

Art: *Alexander the Great Kneeling Before Shimon Hatzaddik* by Zvi Raphaeli (https://www.mutualart.com/Artwork/Alexander-the-Great-Kneeling-before-Shim/8BDF6BCF8B926D31)

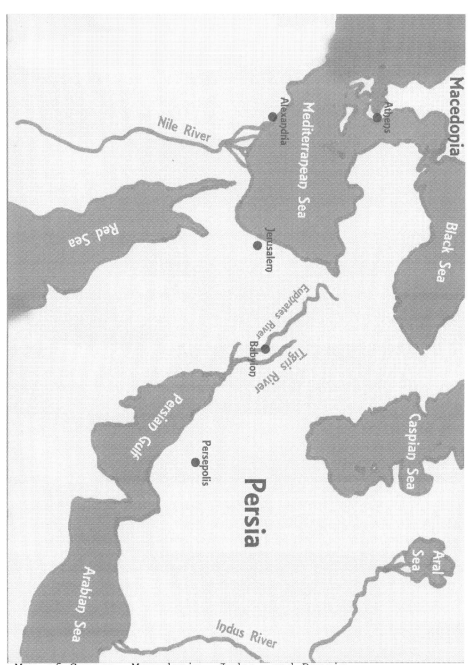

Map of Greece, Macedonia, Judea, and Persia

Week 1

From: *True Gift*, by Yehudis Litvak

Copy work/dictation passage:

Leah picked up another piece of reed from the quickly dwindling pile in front of her. The reed smelled fresh, full of promise, and felt smooth and pliable in her hand. She inserted one end into the opening of the basket skeleton she was holding, and quickly pulled it through, in and out. The basket was taking shape, slowly but surely. Glinting in the sun, it almost looked like real gold.

Underline the subjects of the simple sentences in this paragraph.

Week 2

From: *In Every Generation*, by Yehudis Litvak

Copy work/dictation passage:

The papyrus letter with a Persian seal looked to Nachum like an arrow aimed straight for his heart. Nachum read the letter once, twice, and then buried his head in his hands. Had it really come to this? After decades of peace under the Persian rule, was his beloved Eretz Yisrael on the verge of war? And if so, whose side should the Jews take?

Underline all nouns and label them as abstract, proper, or common.

Week 3

From: *Brotherly Love,* by Yehudis Litvak

Copy work/dictation passage:

But jealousy can do this to people. And if this is what happened to Chonio, who didn't even seek honor, can you imagine how powerful jealousy can be for ambitious people who run after honor? It can ruin their lives.

Underline nouns with derivational suffixes. Circle the suffixes.

Month 2

Overview

As families are still adjusting to this curriculum, and perhaps catching up from the Tishrei holidays, this month only contains three weeks of work. As usual, if you find yourself with extra time, please use the additional recommended reading, or focus on another subject that your children are particularly interested in.

Focus of the month: Judea under Ptolemaic rule

Events: division of Alexander's empire after his death; the Ptolemy dynasty; the Septuagint

Time period: years 3460 - 3560 on the Jewish calendar (years 301 - 201 BCE)

Brief summary of the time period:

After Alexander the Great dies unexpectedly, his empire is divided among three of his generals. Judea falls to Ptolemy, the ruler of Egypt. While the Syrian ruler fights the Egyptian ruler for Judea, it remains under Egyptian control for a hundred years.

One of the Egyptian kings, Ptolemy II, orders that the Torah be translated into Greek. This translation is called the Septuagint.

Materials

Recommended reading for this month:
　　Ptolemaic Judea by Malkie Swidler

Weekly reading:

　　Week 1: *Royal Reward*, by Yehudis Litvak
　　Week 2: *The Secret Ingredient,* by Yehudis Litvak
　　Week 3: Gemara Sukkah 51b: Synagogue in Alexandria

Grammar: *A Journey Through Grammar Land, Parts 1 and 2* by Jones & Jensen
　　Chapters 3: Substitute Namers (alias Pronouns); and 4: The Simple Naming Part (alias Simple Subject)

Geography:
　　Map of Egypt and Judea
　　Map work: circle Jerusalem; circle Alexandria; trace a route from Alexandria to Jerusalem

Music: *Mar'eh Kohen* —part of Yom Kippur liturgy based on the writings of Ben Sirah (many versions; free version available at https://www.youtube.com/watch?v=K8QUI8jcKB4)

Art: *Library of Alexandria* by O. Von Corven (available at
https://en.wikipedia.org/wiki/Library_of_Alexandria#/media/File:Ancientlibraryalex.jpg)

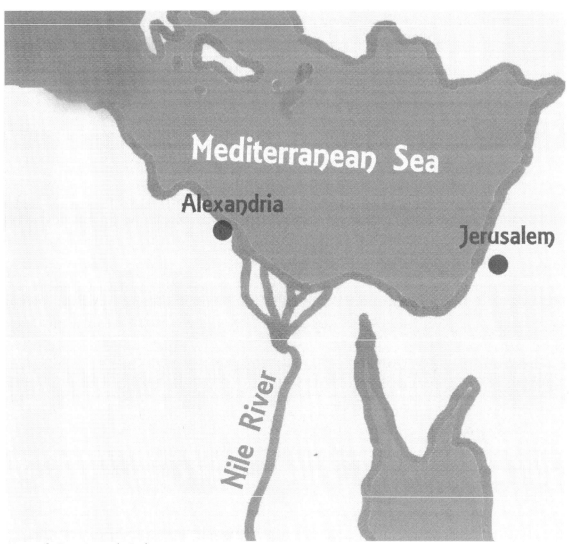

Map of Egypt and Judea

Week 1

From: *Royal Reward*, by Yehudis Litvak

Copy work/dictation passage:

Iosephos had seen holy scrolls in the synagogue in Alexandria. Written in strange letters, which his father had called Hebrew, they certainly weren't anything Iosephos could read. How he'd wished that he could find out what those mysterious scrolls said.

Underline all pronouns and specify if they are nominative, accusative, or possessive.

Week 2

From: *The Secret Ingredient,* by Yehudis Litvak

Copy work/dictation passage:

The scents of the various herbs under his feet tickled Efraim's nostrils when he reached a familiar clearing in the woods. He squinted as the sunlight fell on his face, and looked down at the grass, of all shapes and various shades of green. This was the place. He turned to his son.

In each sentence, underline the simple subject with a single line and the complete subject with a double line.

Week 3

From: Gemara Sukkah 51b

Copy work: the second paragraph in the excerpt below.

You can copy the text from a Gemara (or from Sefaria.org) in the original Hebrew.
If you prefer English, here is a translation from Sefaria.org:

It is taught: Rabbi Yehuda says: One who did not see the great synagogue of Alexandria of Egypt never saw the glory of Israel. They said that its structure **was like a large basilica,** with **a colonnade within a colonnade. At times there were six hundred thousand** men **and** another **six hundred thousand** men **in it, twice the number of those who left Egypt. In it there were seventy-one golden chairs, corresponding to the seventy-one** members **of the Great Sanhedrin, each of which** consisted of **no less than twenty-one thousand talents of gold. And** there was **a wooden platform at the center. The sexton of the synagogue** would **stand on it, with the scarves in his hand. And** because the synagogue was so large and the people could not hear the communal prayer, **when** the prayer leader **reached** the conclusion of a blessing requiring the people **to answer amen,** the sexton **waved the scarf and all the people** would **answer amen.**

And the members of the various crafts **would not sit mingled. Rather, the goldsmiths** would sit **among themselves, and the silversmiths among themselves, and the blacksmiths**

among themselves, and the coppersmiths among themselves, and the weavers among themselves. And when a poor stranger entered there, he would recognize people who plied his craft, and he would turn to join them there. And from there he would secure his livelihood as well as the livelihood of the members of his household, as his colleagues would find him work in that craft.

What was special about the Alexandrian synagogue?

Month 3

Overview

Focus of the month: The Jewish-Greek conflict; the Maccabees
Events: persecution under Syrian-Greeks; Maccabean revolt; rededication of the Temple; Judea becomes independent
Time period: years 3560 - 3625 on the Jewish calendar (years 201 - 134 BCE)

Brief summary of the time period:

The Syrian ruler wrestles Judea away from the Egyptian Ptolemy dynasty. Judea becomes more Hellenized. Antiochus IV issues decrees prohibiting Jewish observance. The Jews, led by the Chashmonai family, revolt, win the war, and gain political independence.

Materials

Recommended reading for this month:

The Miracles of Chanuka Then and Now by Genendel Krohn, Section 1

Additional reading:

Elementary:
The Stone of the Altar by Meir Baram

Middle grades/high school:
In Those Days In This Time by Etka Gitel Schwartz
The Above Reason trilogy: *Swords and Scrolls*, *Spies and Scholars*, and *Secret and Sacred* by Yehudis Litvak

Weekly reading:

Week 1: *Young Hasmoneans,* by Nissan Mindel
Week 2: *The Makings of a Miracle,* by Yehudis Litvak
Week 3: *The Recruit,* by Rabbi Solomon Alter Halpern
Week 4: *Al Hanissim* (according to tradition, composed and added to prayers by Yochanan Kohen Gadol shortly after these events)

Grammar: *A Journey Through Grammar Land, Parts 1 and 2* by Jones & Jensen
Chapter 5: The Complete Telling Part (alias Complete Predicate)

Geography:

Map of Syria and Judea
Map work: circle Jerusalem; circle Antiochia; trace a route from Antiochia to
Jerusalem

Music: *Maoz Tzur* (many versions; free version available at
https://www.chabad.org/multimedia/music_cdo/aid/104615/jewish/Maoz-Tzur.htm)

Art: Bust of King Antiochus:
https://en.wikipedia.org/wiki/Antiochus_IV_Epiphanes#/media/File:Antiochus_IV_Epiphanes_-
_Altes_Museum_-_Berlin_-_Germany_2017.jpg

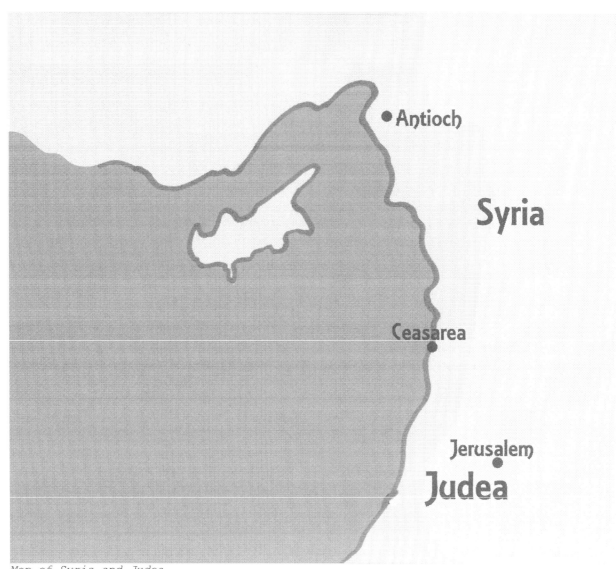

Map of Syria and Judea

Week 1

From: *Young Hasmoneans,* by Nissan Mindel

Copy work/dictation passage:

The sound of cautious steps reached their ears. Their hearts began to beat faster. But then they saw the reassuring wave of a hand; it was their watchman's signal that all was well. Presently, Ovadia appeared.

In each sentence, underline the complete predicate.

Week 2

From: *The Makings of a Miracle,* by Yehudis Litvak

Copy work/dictation passage:

The next several hours were a blur. Tirtza ran back and forth from the cellar, bringing the cheeses and the aged wine Maras Yehudis had asked for. In the kitchen, everything was flying as Maras Yehudis prepared her famous cheese pastries. Tirtza remembered with a pang that she hadn't seen her mistress bake her specialties ever since the master, Mar Menashe, had died.

Underline all verbs. Label them as active or linking verbs.

Week 3

From: *Choni the Circle Maker* from Gemara Taanis 19a; available in English translation at https://www.chabad.org/library/article_cdo/aid/448345/jewish/Choni-the-Circle-Maker.htm

Copy work/dictation:

Choni prayed, but no rain fell. What did he do? He drew a circle, stood inside it, and said to G-d: "Master of the Universe! Your children turned to me because I am like a member of Your household. I swear by Your great name that I'm not budging from here until You have compassion on Your children!"

Pay attention to punctuation. Do an oral narration of the passage.

Week 3

From: *The Recruit,* by Rabbi Solomon Alter Halpern.

Copy work/dictation passage:

And fight he did — from the ambush actions to the pitched battle in which the Syrian army was beaten, and on to Jerusalem where they drove the garrison from the Temple area. As he helped to pull down the idols that had been put there, he remembered how he had torn down the Greek lies within his own mind. As he learnt of the miracle of the lights, he knew that the light of the Torah would never be extinguished, but would one day illuminate the whole world.

Underline all verbs with a single line, and verbs with derivational suffixes with a double line.

Week 4

From: The prayer of *Al Hanissim*

Copy work: The first paragraph below

You can copy the text from a *siddur* (or from sefaria.org) in the original Hebrew. If you prefer English, here is a translation from sefaria.org (slightly edited):

Upon the miracles, and upon the redemption, and upon the mighty acts, and for salvation, and for the wonders, and for the comfort that you did for our fathers in those days at this time.

In the days of Matitya son of Yohanan, the high priest, the Hashmonay and his sons, when the wicked Greek empire arose against Your people Israel, to make them forget Your Torah, and to remove them from the ordinances of Your will, and You with Your great mercy stood at the time of their suffering , You battled their battles, You judged their laws, You took vengeance upon their vengeance, You gave over the mighty into the hands of the weak, and the masses in the hands of the few, and the impure into the hands of the pure, and the wicked into the hands of the righteous, and the intentional sinners into the hands of those that are engaged in your Torah. To You You made Your holy and great name in Your world, and for Your people Israel You made a great salvation and deliverance as You do this day. And afterward, Your children came to the inner chambers of Your house, cleared Your sanctuary, and purified Your holy Temple, and lit candles in Your holy courtyard. And they fixed these eight days of Hanukkah – with complete praise and thanks, and You did for them miracles and wonders, and we will thank Your great name, forever.

Do an oral narration of this prayer.

Month 4

Overview

Focus of the month: the Chashmonai dynasty
Events: Judea under Chashmonai rulers; internal strife; divide between Pharisees and Sadducees
Time period: years 3625 - 3725 on the Jewish calendar (years 134 - 37 BCE)

Brief summary of the time period:

Under the leadership of Yochanan Hyrkanos Judea expands and prospers. Unfortunately, while at peace with its enemies, Judea now has a new challenge — internal strife. Yochanan himself has to fight his brother-in-law for the throne. Besides, his conquests and his insistence that the conquered people convert to Judaism meet with criticism from the rabbis and religious leaders. A new religious group, the Sadducees, arises and grows to prominence. They reject the Oral Torah and the authority of the rabbis. Hungry for power and wealth, they ingratiate themselves to the Chashmonai rulers and turn them against the rabbis. Sadly, this political move results in massacres of the rabbis and their supporters, and eventually to civil war.

Materials

Recommended reading for this month:
The Chashmonai Dynasty, by Malkie Swidler

Weekly reading:

Week 1: *The War for Peace,* by Yehudis Litvak
Week 2: *Lost and Found,* by Yehudis Litvak
Week 3: *Choni the Circle Maker* from Gemara Taanis 19a; available in English translation at https://www.chabad.org/library/article_cdo/aid/448345/jewish/Choni-the-Circle-Maker.htm
Week 4: *Growing with Barley,* by Yehudis Litvak

Grammar: *A Journey Through Grammar Land, Parts 1 and 2* by Jones & Jensen
Chapter 6: Tellers (alias Verbs)

Geography:

Map of the Land of Israel
Map work: color the territory of Judea before Yochanan Hyrknanos's conquests in one color; color the territories he added in a different color

Music: *Adventures in the Beis Hamikdash* by Yerucham Levin; series of albums, available at https://www.galpazmusic.com/

Art: Coins from the reign of Yochanan Hyrkanus:
https://en.wikipedia.org/wiki/John_Hyrcanus#/media/File:John_Hyrcanus.jpg

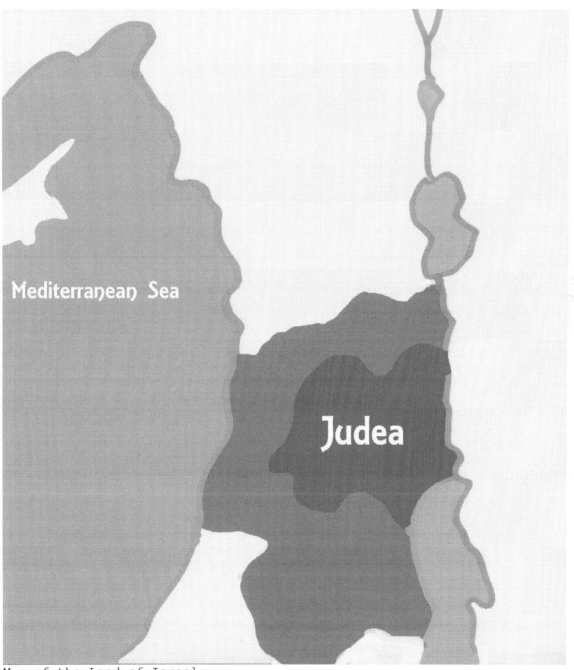

Map of the Land of Israel

Week 1

From: *The War for Peace,* by Yehudis Litvak

Copy work/dictation passage:

"Quality weapons you have," he said. Handing the sword back to Zerach, he ordered, "Show me how you use it." When Zerach looked at him questioningly, he explained, "If my son is going to fight, it is my duty as a father to make sure he knows how."

Underline all the verbs in present tense and mark them with the correct form: first person present, third person singular present, or present participle.

Week 2

From: *Lost and Found,* by Yehudis Litvak

Copy work/dictation passage:

They left right after breakfast and walked as fast as they could, stopping for the night in small Jewish villages along the way. The journey took several days. Everyone was tearful when they crossed the border of Eretz Yisrael into Syria. Yehoshua swallowed a lump in his throat as the last Jewish settlements in the north of Eretz Yisrael slowly faded from view.

Underline all verbs and label them as regular or irregular.

Week 3

From: *Lost and Found,* by Yehudis Litvak

Copy work/dictation passage: *Choni the Circle Maker* from Gemara Taanis 19a; available in English translation at
https://www.chabad.org/library/article_cdo/aid/448345/jewish/Choni-the-Circle-Maker.htm

Choni prayed, but no rain fell. What did he do? He drew a circle, stood inside it, and said to G-d: "Master of the Universe! Your children turned to me because I am like a member of Your household. I swear by Your great name that I'm not budging from here until You have compassion on Your children!"

Do an oral narration of the story.

Week 4

From: *Growing with Barley,* by Yehudis Litvak

Copy work/dictation passage:

Elazar saw a sea of green barley stalks swaying in the breeze. Coming closer, he grasped a barley stalk with his fingers. The kernels felt strong, solid, healthy. They were almost ripe. After Pesach, they could be harvested. But first, before anyone could partake of the new crop, the korban haomer needed to be brought. Elazar's heart swelled. It was his field, his barley, that made the new harvest permissible to all of the Jewish people.

Underline all verb clusters.

Month 5

Overview

Focus of the month: Rome takes control over Judea
Events: King Herod; persecution of the Sages; Herod rebuilds the Temple; Hillel and Shammai
Time period: years 3725 - 3827 on the Jewish calendar (years 37 BCE - 67 CE)

Brief summary of the time period:

The unrest in Judea turns into a civil war when two Chashmonai brothers, Hyrkanus and Aristobulus, fight for the throne. Eventually, the brothers turn to Rome, a new rising power, to mediate their dispute.

Rome is happy to oblige, taking advantage of the situation to slowly gain control over Judea. Eventually, with Rome's approval, Herod rises to power. After more internal fighting, Herod becomes king over Judea. He murders the Chashmonai family and the Sages of the Sanhedrin. Later, he regrets his deeds. As a compensation to the Jewish people, he rebuilds the Temple, making it more magnificent than ever before.

While Herod is busy with political leadership, two rabbis, Hillel and Shammai, become the religious leaders of Judea. Respected by everyone, including Herod himself, they build up their respective schools and strengthen Torah learning and observance in the land.

Materials

Recommended reading for this month:
Judea under the Romans, by Malkie Swidler

Additional reading:

Elementary:
On One Foot by Linda Glaser
High school:
Ithamar by Marcus Lehmann

Weekly reading:

Week 1: *In Pursuit of Justice,* by Yehudis Litvak
Week 2: *Changing Course,* by Yehudis Litvak
Week 3: *From Matzah to Chametz,* by Yehudis Litvak
Week 4: *To Remain Free,* by Yehudis Litvak

Grammar: *A Journey Through Grammar Land, Parts 3 and 4* by Jones & Jensen
Chapter 7: Descriptive Mountains, Home of the Limiters (alias Adjectives)

Geography:
Map of the Land of Israel and Rome

Map work: trace a sea route from Rome to the Land of Israel

Music: *Hillel's Song* by Ma Tovuh:
https://music.amazon.com/albums/B00129RZK6?trackAsin=B00129RZAG&do=play&ref=dm_ws_dp_sp_bb_phfs_xx_xx

Art: Model of Herod's Temple:
https://en.wikipedia.org/wiki/Holyland_Model_of_Jerusalem#/media/File:Jerusalem_Modell_BW_2.JPG

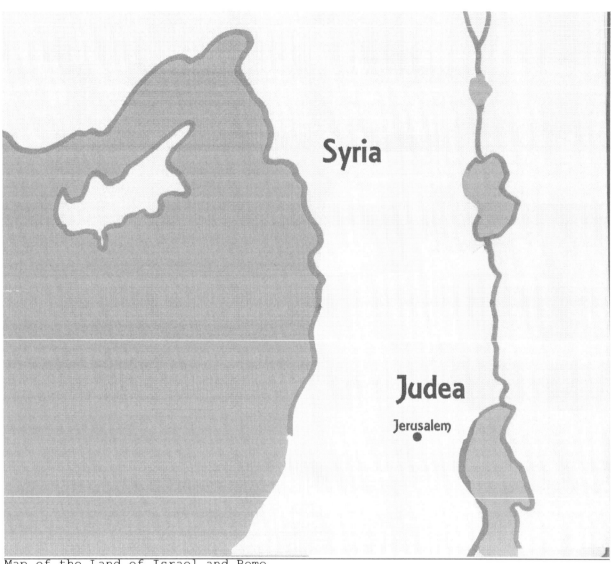

Map of the Land of Israel and Rome

Week 1

From: *In Pursuit of Justice,* by Yehudis Litvak

Copy work/dictation passage:

Over the next few days, delegation after delegation arrived from Galil, seeking a meeting with Hyrkanos himself. Community leaders, as well as relatives of the murdered young men, urged Hyrkanos to bring Herod to trial. Gamliel thought his heart would break when he saw Naftali's mother, with red eyes and puffy face. Together with the other bereaved mothers, she met with Hyrkanus. Perhaps the mothers broke Hyrkanus's heart too, because the next day the king sent a summons to Herod.

Underline all adjectives and mark one of the three ways in which they describe: 1) what kind; 2) which one; or 3) how many.

Week 2

From: *Changing Course,* by Yehudis Litvak

Copy work/dictation passage:

Overcome by tremendous joy, Menashe felt his doubts melt inside him. From now on, he would be a different person. He would live a simpler lifestyle and devote his time to studying the Oral Torah. His father wouldn't be happy. His friends might reject him. But this world wasn't meant to be comfortable. It was a passageway to the World to Come, and Menashe was ready for the journey.

Underline adjectives that were made from nouns or verbs.

Week 3

From: *From Matzah to Chametz,* by Yehudis Litvak

Copy work/dictation passage:

With each practice round, Yair found it easier to keep up. Nechunia also kept up, even with the older, more experienced kohanim.

When Uncle Elkana announced a break, Yair led Nechunia outside, to the steps of the Cheil surrounding the Beis Hamikdash. They washed their hands, sat down, and unwrapped their lunches. As Yair chewed on his piece of bread, he watched Nechunia out of the corner of his eye. Nechunia ate slowly and quietly. He seemed deep in thought.

Underline all adjectives in comparative form.

Week 4

From: *To Remain Free,* by Yehudis Litvak

Copy work/dictation passage:

The wheat stalks, green with a hint of gold, stood tall and proud in the light spring breeze. Feeling the sun's warm rays on his back, Uziel took off his cloak and threw it over his shoulder. He breathed in, savoring the smell of the blossoming fruit trees near his family's field, and then took off at a run up the hill toward his home. His parents would be happy to hear his glowing report on the wheat crops, which should be ready to harvest right after Pesach.

Underline all adjectives and specify if they are predicate adjectives or adjective subject complement.

Month 6

Overview

Focus of the month: destruction of the Second Temple

Events: the Roman army besieges Jerusalem; fractured community; internal strife; destruction of the Temple

Time period: years 3827 - 3830 on the Jewish calendar (years 67-70 CE)

Brief summary of the time period:

Judea is now fully under Roman control. The Roman procurators oppress the people of Judea, and there is growing unrest among them. Some try to negotiate with the Romans while others rebel and fight. The Romans move to suppress the rebellion. They destroy many Jewish towns and villages and lay siege to Jerusalem.

However, inside Jerusalem, different factions are busy fighting among themselves. After a long siege, the Romans enter the city, massacre its inhabitants, and destroy the Temple, which had been the center of religious life until then.

A small group of rabbis, headed by Rabban Yochanan ben Zakkai, escape to Yavneh and attempt to revive and revitalize Jewish life in the absence of the Temple.

Materials

Recommended reading for this month:

When We Left Yerushalayim by Genendel Krohn, section 2
Sand and Stars, Volume 1, chapter 1

Additional reading:

Elementary/middle grades:
    The Kingdom Didn't Fall by Meir Baram
High school:
    The Harp by Rabbi Meir Uri Gottesman
    Chains by Leah Gebber

Weekly reading:

Week 1: *The Long Net,* by Rabbi Salomon Alter Halpern
Week 2: *My Cow Broke a Leg,* by Rabbi Salomon Alter Halpern
Week 3: *Perilous Journey,* by Yehudis Litvak
Week 4: *Start of a War,* by Rabbi Salomon Alter Halpern

Grammar: *A Journey Through Grammar Land, Parts 3 and 4* by Jones & Jensen

Chapter 8: Central Intelligence Adverbial Agency, Home of the Clarifiers and Intensifiers (alias Adverbs)

Geography:
 Map of the Land of Israel
 Map work: find and circle Jerusalem

Music: *Eicha* by Sam Glaser: https://www.youtube.com/watch?v=31DQ4zwU6U0

Art: Arch of Titus:
https://en.wikipedia.org/wiki/Second_Temple#/media/File:Rom,_Titusbogen,_Triumphzug_3.jpg

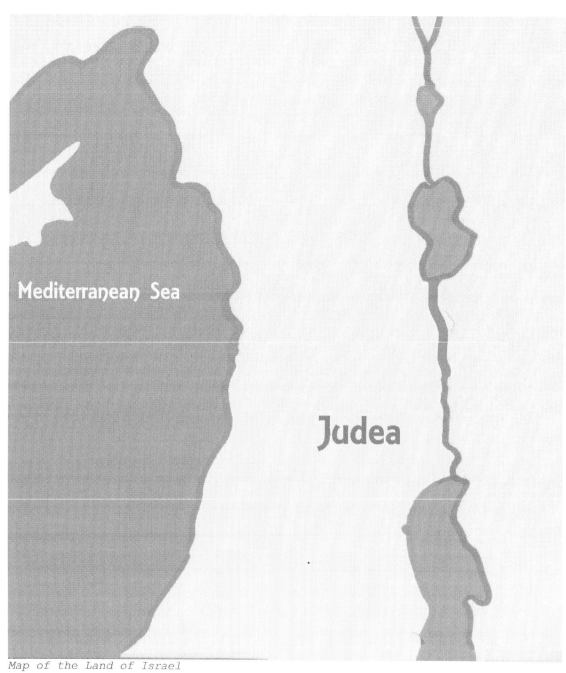

Map of the Land of Israel

Week 1

From: *The Long Net,* by Rabbi Salomon Alter Halpern.

Copy work/dictation passage:

Rabbi Yehuda had motioned his guests to let him deal with the man. He had thought quickly. Here was a man who had committed a great crime, quite without compunction and with great daring. He must be familiar with Jewish laws and customs sufficiently to pass himself off as a Jew — after all, strange-looking Jews from many countries, speaking all sorts of languages, came up to Jerusalem; they could not examine everyone.

Underline all adverbs and specify if they answer 1) when; 2) how; or 3) where.

Week 2

From: *My Cow Broke a Leg,* by Rabbi Salomon Alter Halpern

Copy work/dictation passage:

The autumn sun was peeping over a distant hill in Judaea that was still a self-governing province, though the skeptics said that Rome was only awaiting the end of her northern campaigns to crush her unruly vassal.

Underline all adverbs and specify if they were formed from adjectives or verbs.

Week 3

From: *Perilous Journey,* by Yehudis Litvak

Copy work/dictation passage (page 65):

The boat slowed down. Other boats were now visible, some sailing towards Alexandria and others away from it. One boat caught Amram's attention because it was not moving, but sitting almost still out in the open sea. Its flag, with the emblem of the Roman Empire, was quivering in the breeze.

Underline all adverbs that function as intensifiers.

Week 4

From: *Start of a War,* by Rabbi Salomon Alter Halpern

Copy work/dictation passage:

Slowly Bar Kamtza walked out. Surely all could see that the other man was behaving badly, surely someone would intervene, protest against this outrage!
But everyone stood still, looking the other way.
Hardly was he out of the door, when conversation and music started again.

Underline all adverbs. Do an oral narration of the story.

Month 7

Overview

This is the seventh month of the homeschooling year. If you are beginning your year in the fall, you will be busy preparing for Pesach (see our Jewish Year guide for more details).

Even if you begin your year in a different month, you might want to slow down and reassess how the learning is going, or you might want to review what you covered in the previous months. Therefore, for this month, we prepared only three weeks of learning. As always, if you find yourself with extra time, please see our recommendations for additional reading.

Focus of the month: the first Tannaim
Events: Yavneh and its Sages; Rabbi Akiva; the Bar Kochba revolt
Time period: years 3830 - 3900 on the Jewish calendar (years 70 - 140 CE)

Brief summary of the time period:

The yeshiva in Yavneh is headed by Rabban Gamliel. Under his leadership, many disputes are settled and the foundation of rabbinical Judaism is laid. Other rabbis also influence not only their local communities, but the course of Judaism in history. Among them is Rabbi Akiva.

   The Romans continue persecuting the Jews. When Emperor Hadrian outlaws such basics of Judaism as Shabbos and circumcision, the Jews, led by Shimon Bar Kochba, revolt against Roman rule. At first, the rebellion succeeds, and for two years, the Judea again becomes an independent state. But eventually the Romans bring additional forces into Judea and defeat the Jewish rebels, massacring hundreds of thousands of Jews.

Materials

Recommended reading for this month:
    Sand and Stars, Volume 1, chapters 2 and 3

Additional reading:

    Elementary:
        Drop by Drop: Story of Rabbi Akiva by Jacqueline Hechtkopf

    Middle grades/high school:
        And Rachel Was His Wife

Weekly reading:

    Week 1: *Friends and Foes,* by Yehudis Litvak
    Week 2: *A Star Shall Rise From Yaakov*, by Yehudis Litvak
    Week 3: *The Fox and the Fish*, available at
https://www.chabad.org/library/article_cdo/aid/2872/jewish/The-Fox-and-the-Fishes.htm

Grammar: *A Journey Through Grammar Land, Parts 3 and 4* by Jones & Jensen
    Chapter 9: Prepositional Railway Yard, Home of the Matchmakers (alias Prepositions)

Geography:
    Map of the Land of Israel
    Map work: find and circle Yavneh and Beitar

Music: *Amar Rabbi Akiva Ve'ahavta* (many versions; free version available at http://www.zemirotdatabase.org/view_song.php?id=230)

Art: Bar Kochba coins:
https://en.wikipedia.org/wiki/Second_Temple#/media/File:Barkokhba-silver-tetradrachm.jpg

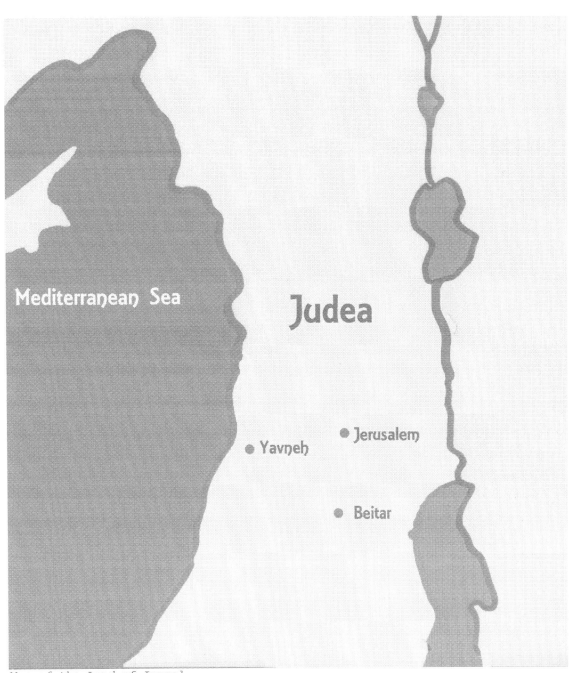

Map of the Land of Israel

Week 1

From: *Friends and Foes,* by Yehudis Litvak

Copy work/dictation passage:

When other men came to relieve the guards, Todros followed the guard who'd offered to help him. Again, they took a twisted and confusing path through narrow alleys, and Todros soon gave up on remembering the way. On the way, the Biryoni kept boasting about his exploits outside the city to cause damage to the Romans. Todros just listened and nodded. While the Biryoni's victories were impressive, they paled in comparison to the might of the Roman army.

Underline all prepositional phrases.

Week 2

From: *A Star Shall Rise from Yaakov*, by Yehudis Litvak

Copy work/dictation passage:

Chanina followed Shmuel into the depths of the cave. He had to bend his head and almost crawl through narrow tunnels until they came to a wide space lit up with numerous torches lined along the cave walls.

Underline all prepositions and specify if they are time or space relational.

Week 3

From: *The Fox and the Fish*, available at
https://www.chabad.org/library/article_cdo/aid/2872/jewish/The-Fox-and-the-Fishes.htm

Copy work/dictation passage:

"Said they to him: 'Are you the one of whom it is said that you are the wisest of animals? You're not wise, but foolish! If, in our environment of life we have cause for fear, how much more so in the environment of our death!'

Pay attention to punctuation. Do an oral narration of the story.

Month 8

Overview

This is the eighth month of the homeschooling year. If you are beginning your year in the fall, you will be busy celebrating Pesach (see our Jewish Year guide for more details).

Even if you begin your year in a different month, you might want to slow down and reassess how the learning is going, or you might want to review what you covered in the previous months. Therefore, for this month, we prepared only three weeks of learning. As always, if you find yourself with extra time, please see our recommendations for additional reading.

Focus of the month: The compilation of the Mishna

Events: Rabbi Shimon bar Yochai; death of Hadrian and relative calm in Judea; Rabbi Yehuda Hanasi; Mishna

Time period: years 3900 - 3960 on the Jewish calendar (years 140 - 200 CE)

Brief summary of the time period:

Emperor Hadrian outlawed teaching Torah in public and murdered most rabbis. Rabbi Shimon bar Yochai, one of the prominent rabbis of the time, was forced into hiding. Other rabbis managed to escape to Babylonia.

After Hadrian's death, relative calm returned to Judea. Recognizing the situation as a brief reprieve, Rabbi Yehuda Hanasi used the opportunity to compile and redact the Mishna - a text we study till this day.

Materials

Recommended reading for this month:
    Sand and Stars, Volume 1, chapters 4 and 5

Additional reading:

    Elementary:
      The Story of Rabbi Shimon Bar Yochai by Genendel Krohn
      Tallis Ends and Other Tales by Rabbi Don Channen

    Weekly reading:

      Week 1: *The Good Medicine*, by Yocheved Segal (Our Sages Showed the Way, Volume 1)
      Week 2: *Six Hundred Dinars Minus Six*, available at https://www.chabad.org/library/article_cdo/aid/293978/jewish/Six-Hundred-Dinars-Minus-Six.htm
      Week 3: *Treating Others Nicely*, by Yocheved Segal (Our Sages Showed the Way, Volume 1)

    Grammar: *A Journey Through Grammar Land, Parts 3 and 4* by Jones & Jensen

Chapter 10: Connection Junction, Home of the Coordinating Conjunctions (alias FANBOYS)

Geography:
Map of the Land of Israel
Map work: find and circle Usha, Tzippori, and Tveria

Music: *Lag Baomer B'Meron* album by Shmili Binyomin (available at https://music.amazon.com/albums/B07CW1DYJ7?tab=CATALOG&ref=dm_wcp_albm_link_pr_s)

Art: Menucha Yankelevitch's art: Tombs of the Tzaddikim: http://menuchay.com/english/gallery/Biblical_figures/

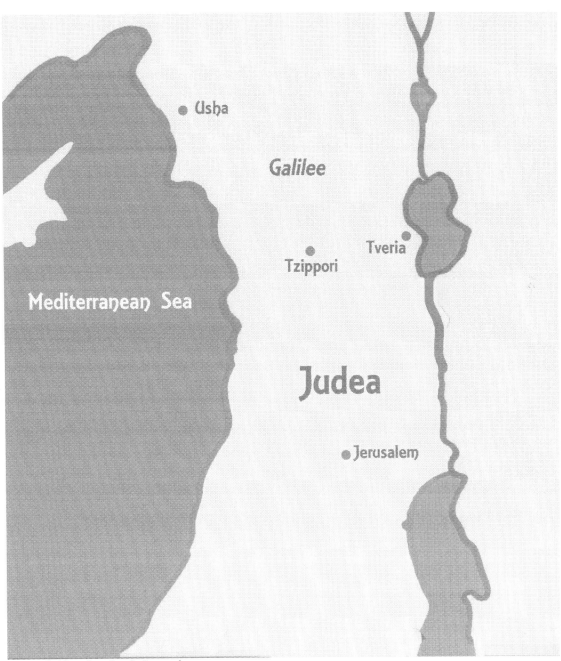

Map of the Land of Israel

Week 1

From: *The Good Medicine*, by Yocheved Segal (Our Sages Showed the Way, Volume 1)

Copy work/dictation passage:

Once, the peddler came to the city where Rabbi Yannai, a great rabbi, lived. Rabbi Yannai sat in his house, which was on the second floor, and learned Torah all day long. When he heard the peddler calling out for people to buy his wonderful medicine so that they could live long, he was curious just like everyone else.

Underline prepositions that govern objective cases with two lines and the objective cases themselves with one line.

Week 2

From: *Six Hundred Dinars Minus Six*, available at
https://www.chabad.org/library/article_cdo/aid/293978/jewish/Six-Hundred-Dinars-Minus-Six.htm

Copy work/dictation passage:

Almost a year later they had another strange visit—from a posse of Roman soldiers with an order for their arrest. Someone accused them of selling silk without paying the tax to the government. They began weeping and protesting their innocence but to no avail.

Do an oral narration of the story.

Week 3

1)   From: *Treating Others Nicely*, by Yocheved Segal (Our Sages Showed the Way, Volume

Copy work/dictation passage:

Finally, they got to Rabbi Shimon's city. People had heard that he was coming back, and they came to greet him and escort him, since he was a very important Torah sage.

Underline all conjunctions.

Month 9

Overview

Focus of the month: Early Amoraim

Events: decline in conditions in Judea; shift of Torah learning to Babylonia; the yeshivos in Babylonia; beginnings of Gemara

Time period: years 3960 - 4210 on the Jewish calendar (years 200 - 350 CE)

Brief summary of the time period:

Due to unrest and physical devastation in Judea, many of its residents leave for better opportunities. Torah learning slowly shifts to the yeshivos in Babylonia, which had existed throughout the Second Temple period. Now, they take center stage in the development of Jewish texts. The Babylonian rabbis begin their work on Gemara, an elucidation of the Mishna.

At the same time, the remaining rabbis in the Land of Israel begin work on Gemara Yerushalmi, the Jerusalem Talmud.

Materials

Recommended reading for this month:
Sand and Stars, volume 1, chapter 6

Weekly reading:

Week 1: *A Load of Scrolls*, by Yehudis Litvak
Week 2: *A Mitzvah for Its Own Sake*, by Nissan Mindel, available from
https://www.chabad.org/library/article_cdo/aid/958/jewish/A-Mitzvah-For-Its-Own-Sake.htm
Week 3: *A Secret Gift*, by Yocheved Segal (Our Sages Showed the Way, Volume
1)
Week 4: *Why the Reedcutter Didn't Die*, available from
https://www.chabad.org/library/article_cdo/aid/2832663/jewish/Why-the-Reedcutter-Didnt-Die.htm

Grammar: *A Journey Through Grammar Land, Part 5* by Jones & Jensen
Chapter 11: Thought Trucking Terminal, Home of the Simple Sentence Patterns

Geography:
Map of Babylonia
Map work: find and circle Nehardea and Sura

Music: Rabbi Levi Sudri's *Oral Torah* album: http://www.levisudri.com/songs_en.php

Art: *A Difficult Passage of the Talmud* by Isaac Snowman
https://www.gettyimages.com/detail/news-photo/news-photo/517203300

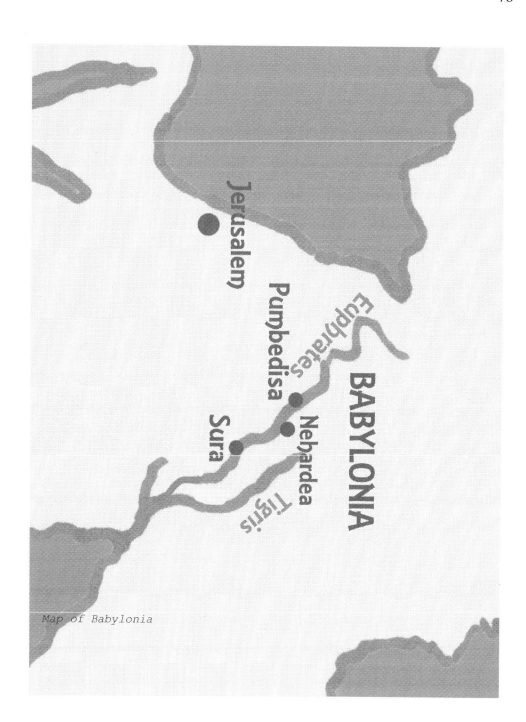

Map of Babylonia

Week 1

From: *A Load of Scrolls*, by Yehudis Litvak

Copy work/dictation passage:

When Nachman picked up the first bag, he realized that the rabbi was not exaggerating. The bag was stuffed with scrolls, and he wondered why the yeshiva students needed so many. Under the rabbi's watchful eyes, he carried the bags carefully into the rabbi's room. His father had given him the largest room in the inn, but even it looked small after Nachman had brought in all the bags.

Underline all the direct objects.

Week 2

From: A Mitzvah for Its Own Sake, by Nissan Mindel, available from
https://www.chabad.org/library/article_cdo/aid/958/jewish/A-Mitzvah-For-Its-Own-Sake.htm

Copy work/dictation passage:

A day passed, and another, and many more. Every day he heard the royal heralds read the proclamation again and again, promising a reward to the finder, or cruel death should he not return it within thirty days. The whole populace of Rome was seething with excitement. Still Rabbi Samuel ben Sosarte held on to the necklace.

Underline each verb and mark it as transitive or intransitive.

Week 3

From: *A Secret Gift*, by Yocheved Segal (Our Sages Showed the Way, Volume 1)

Copy work/dictation passage:

There once lived a great rabbi in Bavel whose name was Mar Ukva. He was busy all the time, either learning Torah or doing mitzvos. He also gave a lot of tzedakah to poor people, but didn't want them to know where the money came from. If they knew who gave them the money, they might be embarrassed to take it. But still, he didn't send it with other people. He went himself, making sure that no one saw him.

Underline all objective case pronouns.

Week 4

From: *Why the Reedcutter Didn't Die*, available from
https://www.chabad.org/library/article_cdo/aid/2832663/jewish/Why-the-Reedcutter-Didnt-Die.htm

Copy work/dictation passage:

The man answered, "Every day, all of us put all our food together and then share it. Today, one man had nothing to share and he was embarrassed, so I told everyone, 'Today I'm going to collect the food.' When I got to him, I pretended to take something from him so that he wouldn't be embarrassed."

Pay attention to punctuation. Do an oral narration of the story.

Month 10

Overview

This is the last month in this time period, and you might want to go over and review what you have learned. We prepared only three weeks of materials. During the last week, you can focus on what you feel needs more attention in the material we've covered. You can also do additional grammar exercises of your choice. Free grammar materials and exercises can be found at https://www.kissgrammar.org/.

Focus of the month: Later Amoraim and completion of the Talmud
Events: completion of the Gemara in Babylonia
Time period: years 4210-4460 on the Jewish calendar (years 350-500 BCE)

Brief summary of the time period:

The subsequent generations of Amoraim continue work on the Talmud, both the Jerusalem and the Babylonian one. As the persecution in Eretz Yisrael intensifies, the traditional determination of the Jewish calendar becomes very difficult. Hillel the Nasi establishes a fixed Jewish calendar for all future generations. By the year 425 CE, the ruling emperor abolishes the office of the Nasi, and the Jews in Eretz Yisrael lose their last vestiges of autonomy. The last yeshivos in Eretz Yisrael are forced to close, thus putting an end to the work on the Jerusalem Talmud.

The increase in anti-Semitism throughout the world brings about the first blood libel, which results in the destruction of the Jewish community in Antioch, Syria. The Jewish community in Alexandria is also destroyed.

Meanwhile, Torah learning in the Babylonian yeshivos continues, with new yeshivos opening up in different locations. Under the leadership of Rav Ashi, the Babylonian Talmud is completed and preserved for future generations.

Towards the end of the 5th century CE, anti-Semitic sentiments reach Bavel. After centuries of peaceful communal life, the Jews find themselves an object of persecution. Three prominent members of the Jewish community are arrested and executed. Jewish children are seized and handed over to Persian priests. Many Jews leave their homes in search of a safer alternative.

Materials

Recommended reading for this month:
Sand and Stars, volume 1, chapter 7

Weekly reading:

Week 1: *A Member of the King's Household*, by Yocheved Segal (Our Sages Showed the Way, Volume 5)
Week 2: *Love of Eretz Yisrael*, by Yocheved Segal (Our Sages Showed the Way, Volume 4)
Week 3: *How to Ask Nicely*, by Yocheved Segal (Our Sages Showed the Way, Volume 5)

Grammar: *A Journey Through Grammar Land, Part 5* by Jones & Jensen
Chapter 12: Clause Village, Home of the Complex Sentence Builders

Geography:
Map of Babylonia
Map work: find and circle Pumbedisa

Music: Amar Rabbi Elazar: https://en.wikipedia.org/wiki/File:Omar_Rabbi_Elozor.ogg

Art: Talmud Readers by Adolf Behrman
(https://en.wikipedia.org/wiki/Mishnah#/media/File:Adolf_Behrman_-_Talmudysci.jpg)

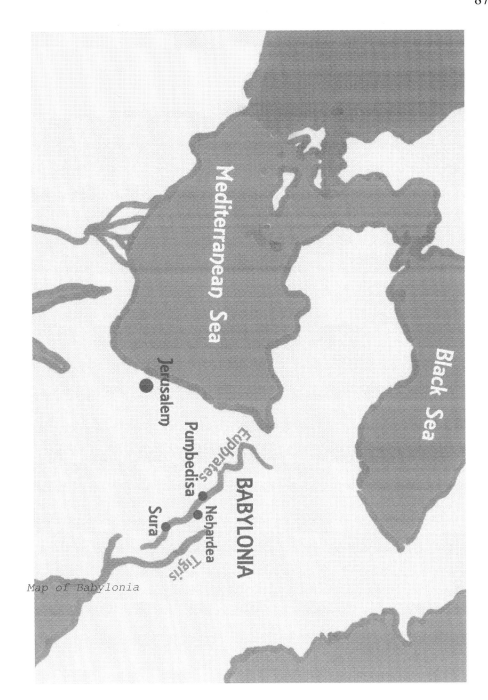

Map of Babylonia

Week 1

From: *A Member of the King's Household*, by Yocheved Segal (Our Sages Showed the Way, Volume 5)

Copy work/dictation passage:

"Please, sir," he began, "I know that I am not a member of your household, as I stated, but I believed in you, that you would ultimately act with mercy and compassion. Had I not made that claim, the soldiers would have beaten me. They would have never believed that I was simply detained in your city for one night due to unfinished business matters. Really, that's all that happened. Had I been able to return home last night, I certainly would have done so."

Underline all complex sentences.

Week 2

From: *Love of Eretz Yisrael*, by Yocheved Segal (Our Sages Showed the Way, Volume 4)

Copy work/dictation passage:

    On his way, Rabbi Zeira came to a river that didn't have a bridge. The ferryboat which normally took the people across the river was nowhere in sight. How would he cross? He spotted a narrow plank which lay across the whole river, and above it was a rope which was tied to posts on either side of the river. This path was for fishermen and workmen who had no time to wait for the ferry. They had been walking back and forth across this plank for many years and it was no longer difficult for them.

Underline all relative clauses.

Week 3

From: *How to Ask Nicely*, by Yocheved Segal (Our Sages Showed the Way, Volume 5)

Copy work/dictation passage:

Rav Acha says: There are women who know how to ask for something and those who don't. A smart woman who needs a sifter, for example, for sifting flour goes to her neighbor to borrow one. She comes to her neighbor's house, and even though the door is wide open, she doesn't enter without permission, for that would be rude. She knocks on the door and waits for her neighbor to come to the door or at least call to her to come in. She then greets her neighbor politely.

Choose a sentence from the above paragraph and label each clause in that sentence.

Appendix A

Required reading

Spine texts:

- *The Miracles of Chanuka Then and Now* by Genendel Krohn
- *When We Left Yerushalayim* by Genendel Krohn
- *Chapters in Jewish History* by Malkie Swidler
- Sand and Stars, Volume 1, by Yaffa Ganz, in collaboration with Rabbi Berel
Wein

Literature:

- *The Prisoner and Other Tales of Faith* by Rabbi Salomon Halpern
- *Stories of the Second Beis Hamikdash* by Yehudis Litvak
- *Stories of the Tannaim* by Yehudis Litvak
- *Eight Chanukah Tales* by Nissan Mindel
- *Our Sages Showed the Way* by Yocheved Segal, volumes 1, 4, and 5

- Selected stories available at chabad.org

Grammar:

- *A Journey Through Grammar Land*, Parts 1 and 2 by Vernie O. Jones and Frode Jensen
- *A Journey Through Grammar Land*, Parts 3 and 4 by Vernie O. Jones and Frode Jensen
- *A Journey Through Grammar Land*, Part 5 by Vernie O. Jones and Frode Jensen

Books for additional reading

Elementary:

- *The Stone of the Altar* by Meir Baram
- *On One Foot* by Linda Glaser
- *The Kingdom Didn't Fall* by Meir Baram
- *Drop by Drop: Story of Rabbi Akiva* by Jacqueline Hechtkopf
- *The Story of Rabbi Shimon Bar Yochai* by Genendel Krohn
- *Tallis Ends and Other Tales* by Rabbi Don Channen

Middle Grades/High School:

- *In Those Days In This Time* by Etka Gitel Schwartz
- The Above Reason trilogy: *Swords and Scrolls*, *Spies and Scholars*, and *Secret and Sacred* by Yehudis Litvak
- *Ithamar* by Marcus Lehmann
- *The Harp* by Rabbi Meir Uri Gottesman
- *Chains* by Leah Gebber
- *And Rachel Was His Wife*

Recommended music

Month 1: *Somachti* by Shalsheles (song # 4 in the album *Connections;* available at https://mostlymusic.com/products/connections)

Month 2: *Mar'eh Kohen* —part of Yom Kippur liturgy based on the writings of Ben Sirah (many versions; free version available at https://www.youtube.com/watch?v=K8QUI8jcKB4)

Month 3: *Maoz Tzur* (many versions; free version available at https://www.chabad.org/multimedia/music_cdo/aid/104615/jewish/Maoz-Tzur.htm)

Month 4: Adventures in the Beis Hamikdash by Yerucham Levin; series of albums, available at https://www.galpazmusic.com/

Month 5: *Hillel's Song* by Ma Tovuh: https://music.amazon.com/albums/B00129RZK6?trackAsin=B00129RZAG&do=play&ref=dm_ws_dp_sp_bb_phfs_xx_xx

Month 6: *Eicha* by Sam Glaser: https://www.youtube.com/watch?v=31DQ4zwU6U0

Month 7: *Amar Rabbi Akiva Ve'ahavta* (many versions; free version available at http://www.zemirotdatabase.org/view_song.php?id=230)

Month 8: *Lag Baomer B'Meron* album by Shmili Binyomin (available at https://music.amazon.com/albums/B07CW1DYJ7?tab=CATALOG&ref=dm_wcp_albm_link_pr_s)

Month 9: Rabbi Levi Sudri's *Oral Torah* album: http://www.levisudri.com/songs_en.php

Month 10: *Amar Rabbi Elazar*: https://en.wikipedia.org/wiki/File:Omar_Rabbi_Elozor.ogg

Recommended art

Month 1: *Alexander the Great Kneeling Before Shimon Hatzaddik* by Zvi Raphaeli (https://www.mutualart.com/Artwork/Alexander-the-Great-Kneeling-before-Shim/8BDF6BCF8B926D31)

Month 2: *Library of Alexandria* by O. Von Corven (https://en.wikipedia.org/wiki/Library_of_Alexandria#/media/File:Ancientlibraryalex.jpg)

Month 3: Bust of King Antiochus: https://en.wikipedia.org/wiki/Antiochus_IV_Epiphanes#/media/File:Antiochus_IV_Epiphanes_-_Altes_Museum_-_Berlin_-_Germany_2017.jpg

Month 4: Coins from the reign of Yochanan Hyrcanus: https://en.wikipedia.org/wiki/John_Hyrcanus#/media/File:John_Hyrcanus.jpg

Month 5: Model of Herod's Temple: https://en.wikipedia.org/wiki/Holyland_Model_of_Jerusalem#/media/File:Jerusalem_Modell_BW_2.JPG

Month 6: Arch of Titus: https://en.wikipedia.org/wiki/Second_Temple#/media/File:Rom,_Titusbogen,_Triumphzug_3.jpg

Month 7: Bar Kochba coins: https://en.wikipedia.org/wiki/Second_Temple#/media/File:Barkokhba-silver-tetradrachm.jpg

Month 8: Menucha Yankelevitch's art: Tombs of the Tzaddikim: http://menuchay.com/english/gallery/Biblical_figures/

Month 9: *A Difficult Passage of the Talmud* by Isaac Snowman
https://www.gettyimages.com/detail/news-photo/news-photo/517203300
Month 10: *Talmud Readers* by Adolf Behrman
(https://en.wikipedia.org/wiki/Mishnah#/media/File:Adolf_Behrman_-_Talmudysci.jpg)

Map list

1)Map of Greece, Macedonia, Judea, and Persia
2) Map of Egypt and Judea
3) Map of Syria and Judea
4) Map of the Land of Israel
5) Map of the Land of Israel and Rome
6) Map of the Land of Israel
7) Map of the Land of Israel
8) Map of the Land of Israel
9) Map of Babylonia
10) Map of Babylonia

Notes

Notes

Made in the USA
Middletown, DE
29 October 2021